WHAT EVERY

Christian Heritage

Developed by the
Christian Education Staff
of The General Board of Discipleship
of The United Methodist Church

DISCIPLESHIP RESOURCES

P.O. BOX 340003 • NASHVILLE, TN 37203-0003
www.discipleshipresources.org

This booklet was developed by the Christian Education Staff of the General Board of Discipleship of The United Methodist Church. It is one in a series of booklets designed to provide essential knowledge for teachers. Members of the staff who helped write and develop this series are Terry Carty, Bill Crenshaw, Donna Gaither, Rick Gentzler, Mary Alice Gran, Susan Hay, Betsey Heavner, Diana Hynson, Carol Krau, MaryJane Pierce Norton, Deb Smith, Julia Wallace, and Linda Whited.

Reprinted 2002, 2003

Cover and book design by Joey McNair
Cover illustration by Mike Drake

Edited by Debra D. Smith and Cindy S. Harris

ISBN 0-88177-364-6

Scripture quotations, unless otherwise indicated, are from the New Revised Standard Version of the Bible, copyright © 1989 by the Division of Christian Education of the National Council of the Churches of Christ in the USA. All rights reserved. Used by permission.

WHAT EVERY TEACHER NEEDS TO KNOW ABOUT CHRISTIAN HERITAGE. Copyright © 2002 Discipleship Resources. All rights reserved. No part of this book may be reproduced in any form whatsoever, print or electronic, without written permission, except in the case of brief quotations embodied in critical articles or reviews. For information regarding rights and permissions, contact Discipleship Resources, P.O. Box 340003, Nashville, TN 37203-0003; phone 800-814-7833 (toll-free) or 615-340-7068; fax 615-340-1789; e-mail mgregory@gbod.org.

DR364

Contents

Introduction 5
God Wants to Be Known 7
God Known by the Ancients. 13
When They Ask 25
Goals of Education 29
Your Place in the Story. 37
Going Further 45
Helpful Resources 47

*This booklet is dedicated to
YOU,
a teacher of
children, youth, or adults,
WHO,
with fear, excitement, joy,
and commitment,
allows God to lead you
in the call to
TEACH.*

*The gifts he gave were that some would be . . .
teachers, . . . for building up the body of Christ.
(Ephesians 4:11-12)*

Introduction

You have accepted a call to teach. You have had plenty of company in this venture through the centuries. Whether you are a teacher of children, youth, or adults, this booklet will help you to understand and appreciate your place in our Christian heritage and to think about your role in passing on the faith.

We begin with the basic premise that God's relationship with us is the core of our being and of the story we tell, so first we must know something about God and how God has been revealed to human beings. You will be invited to reflect on how you have come to know God and what you know and believe about God.

Then we will take a look at the education practices of the early and later faith communities. Why did they teach, and what were their aims? One aim that we share with earlier faith communities is to make disciples. You will consider disciple making and how it fits in with the other aims of the church, such as worship, fellowship, and service.

Following a brief description of Christian education through the church's history, you will be encouraged to think more about your own goals as a teacher and how you would like to pass on the faith to the students in your care. Finally, we will provide some food for future thought: What else can you do or study to help you become equipped for this influential ministry of faith formation and transmission?

This booklet is one of ten that will equip you for teaching. Use the entire series to reinforce your own knowledge, skills, and abilities.

Other booklets in this series are
What Every Teacher Needs to Know About
- *the Bible*
- *Classroom Environment*
- *Curriculum*
- *Faith Language*
- *Living the Faith*
- *People*
- *Teaching*
- *Theology*
- *The United Methodist Church*

God Wants to Be Known

God wants to be known by you and by each of us. Do you remember the story of Moses and the burning bush in Exodus 3? Moses was in Midian minding his sheep and, he thought, minding his own business when he saw a strange phenomenon that riveted his attention. A plant was on fire but was somehow spared from burning to a crisp. When Moses turned aside to have a look, he encountered the God of Abraham, Isaac, and Jacob and was called upon for a huge task: bringing God's name and God's purposes in a new way and at a new time to the Hebrews imprisoned in Egypt. Moses had several excellent excuses not to do so—and pointed out every one of them to God—but God insisted that he go. Moses met God in that fiery shrub, and his life was never the same again.

Or consider the apostle Paul, an ardent and faithful Jew who devoted all his energies to putting an end to the Christian movement (Acts 8:3; 9:1-2)—until God intercepted him on the road to Damascus. Saul, or Paul, was stunned and temporarily blinded by the Spirit of Jesus Christ, who claimed Paul's life as his own (9:3-16). From that moment on, Paul could not do anything other than preach and teach Christ. He met God as if struck by a lightning bolt in the middle of a highway, and Paul's life was never the same again.

Taking a Place in Telling the Story

God takes initiative to be known, as in the burning bush; but God also relies on us to share in that initiative. Telling or teaching others about God is one of the central tasks of education and is at the heart of your call as a teacher.

Passing along the faith has a long history. How else could we follow what the earliest Hebrews or Christians taught so many centuries ago? We may thank our forefathers and foremothers in the faith for taking seriously their responsibility to teach their children and others about God. Now you have joined that long procession to teach the faith to others.

Not Just to Moses and Paul

Throughout all time, God has demonstrated ways of self-revealing and has instructed the faith community to pass along their faith through their own means. We receive, learn about, understand, incorporate, feel, see, and come to know God because God chooses to be known and because others have intentionally taught us about God. We may think of passing on the faith as Christian education, and all Christians have a stake in the success of our educational efforts. As a teacher participating in generation after generation of this long heritage of faith, you have a key role to play with the congregation and other teachers in the spiritual formation and well-being of the people in your care.

Think about who passed on the faith story to you. How did they share stories and beliefs about God?

Think about the way you came to this teaching ministry. Did you volunteer? If so, why? Were you invited? If so, by whom? What were you invited specifically to do? What made you decide to accept?

Did you have serious reservations about the task, like Moses did? If so, what were—or are—they?

Are you eager for this ministry in spite of whatever concerns you may have, like Paul? What excites you the most?

What are your initial thoughts about how to pass on the faith to your students?

God Known by the Ancients

We claim that there is only one God (see Deuteronomy 6:4), but God has an infinite number of ways of being known. Indeed, to try to describe God with just one set of words, images, or descriptors, is to underestimate and undercharacterize God woefully. In order to share God's story with others, we must first have an understanding of how we ourselves conceive of God.

First, look to examples and images from our oldest Scriptures. The ancient Hebrews likened God to a rock (Isaiah 26:4); a stronghold (Nahum 1:7); an eagle (Deuteronomy 32:11-12); a shepherd (Ezekiel 34:15); a refuge (Jeremiah 17:17); a mother (Isaiah 42:14); and many more images from life and nature. The Psalms, for example, offer a rich source of images and characterizations of God and God's interactivity with humankind.

These images, of course, were not just in the imagination of the faithful. These images and characterizations were drawn from the Hebrews' experience of God's activity on their behalf. They affirmed, "The LORD is my shepherd" (Psalm 23:1). We agree because in our life experience God cares for us, protects us, and guides us to safe pasture and still waters. God is described as righteous and just because the oppressed have found vindication in God's commands to the faithful to work for justice (see Isaiah 61).

Think about all the images, metaphors, or characterizations that help you understand who God is or how God is active in your life and in the life of the world. List them here.

Use a Bible dictionary (check with your pastor or church library) to research *God* or *Names of God*, then look up several of the supporting Scripture passages. What are those passages and what images or names are used there?

Which of these images has the greatest meaning for you or touches your own experience the most deeply?

If you do not have a Bible dictionary, skim through the Book of Psalms. What images, metaphors, and characterizations strike you the most deeply? Why?

Consider all these "portraits" of God. How do they help you think about describing God to your students?

God Revealed Through the Christ

God, of course, is revealed and known in different ways throughout the Bible. Some people feel that the God of the Old Testament and the God of the New Testament are somehow different. They reason that God has changed between the testaments, or even that there are two different Gods or versions of the same God. Not so. God is One; God is the Only God.

Each of the testaments employs a different type of literature. The Hebrew Scripture, or what Christians refer to as the Old Testament, includes historical, prophetic, legal, and poetic writings. God is revealed through the Hebrews' long period of development as a people, their captivity and release from Egypt, their acquisition of land, and their fortunes (and misfortunes) at the hands of neighboring nations. It is not unusual to see God portrayed as warrior and king along with the more gentle images of mother and shepherd.

The New Testament reveals God chiefly through the life and ministry of God's Son, Jesus the Christ. Much of the writing is narrative and story, as in the Gospels, or is in the form of correspondence, such as the many letters of Paul. In the Gospel of John, Jesus is shown as a teacher (3:1-21); a prophet (4:7-42); a healer (5:2-18); a friend (11:1-44); and a servant (13:1-20), to name a few characterizations.

In the writings attributed to Paul, Jesus is also seen in a more "cosmic" role, as an exalted figure in the heavens (see 1 Corinthians 15 or Colossians 1:15-23), and as one who brings unity and peace (Ephesians 2:11-22). Jesus Christ frees humanity for fullness and reconciliation (Galatians 3:23-29) and models unity and grace for individuals and for the church (1 Corinthians 12).

Choose one of the Gospels or one of the Letters and skim several chapters, such as Matthew 5–7, Mark 2–3, or Colossians 1–3. What does the passage show you about God?

Look also at your hymnal. Pick out a few of your favorite hymns (and sing them, if you wish). What do they reveal about God? How have hymns or other songs and music helped you form your ideas about God?

As you consider these ways of understanding Jesus, how do they help you imagine how to teach your students about him?

God as Spirit

God is One, but there are many different images of the one God. God is One, but we refer to God as both Father (or Mother) and as Son. God is One, but a third important way to understand God is as the Holy Spirit. Christians are Trinitarians, which means that we accept the idea of "God in three persons, blessed Trinity" (from the hymn "Holy, Holy, Holy!" by Reginald Heber, 1826). The third person, though not an individual in the human sense, is the Spirit. John 14 speaks eloquently about the identity and work of the Holy Spirit, referring to the Spirit as the Advocate, or Comforter, whom God will send after the Crucifixion and Resurrection.

Perhaps the most helpful and important thing Jesus taught his disciples about the Holy Spirit is that the Spirit "will teach you everything, and remind you of all that I have said to you" (John 14:26). You can claim that promise as you pass on the teachings of Jesus to your students. You are never alone when you do God's work. The Spirit is always there to guide you and to help you remember what God would have you do.

Read John 14:18-31. What do these verses teach you about the Holy Spirit?

Look in your hymnal at the affirmations of faith and creeds (*The United Methodist Hymnal*, 880–889). What do they tell you about God in each person of the Trinity?

As you consider these ways of understanding the Holy Spirit, how do they help you imagine how to teach your students about this way of knowing God?

Who Is the God You Know?

Think back now to the experience of Moses or Paul. Some of us have had "burning bush" or "road to Damascus" experiences in which we have dramatically come to know, to know better, or to know differently this awesome God. In those moments, we may have received a clear call to a specific ministry or need. We also know God through a long stream of quiet practices and assurances, such as having grown up in a household that regularly offered prayer and modeled generosity as acts of devotion to God.

Consider again all the ways God is present and known. Think about the most meaningful images of God for you; about the names you give to God and God's activity; about how you have encountered God; about what portrait of God emerges for you through the Old and New Testaments. How do these images and names inspire you?

How do you think God claims your life?

How do these images of God help you think about yourself as one whom God has called and claimed?

How does what you now understand about God revealed to you help shape your understanding of yourself as a teacher who shares these insights with others?

When They Ask

First we come to know God in many ways. Then we share the story, pass on the faith, teach others. Consider how the Old Testament community understood this responsibility.

Our "Marching Orders"

The Hebrews understood themselves to be wholly in God's care. Their identity as a people and as a nation was first communal, not individual. They were the people of God, to whom a land and a faith had been given. This faith is understood through the Law—the first five books of the Bible, known to the Jews as the Torah. The Law taught the Hebrews how to be a holy people, set apart for God and for fulfilling God's purposes. For them, all teaching was religious instruction, teaching them about God and how to be in relationship with God, with neighbor, and with others.

All adults were required to know and observe the Law. They were also expected to teach the Law to their children:

> When your children ask you in time to come, "What is the meaning of the decrees and the statutes and the ordinances that the LORD our God has commanded you?" then you shall say to your children, "We were Pharaoh's slaves in Egypt, but the LORD brought us out of Egypt with a mighty hand."
>
> (See Deuteronomy 6:20-25.)

From the time a boy was able to walk and take his father's hand, he was expected to attend the religious festivals and to learn their importance from his father and the extended community. It was through this teaching, experience, and modeling that the boy's entire life, not just his faith, was formed. By agreeing to teach in the church school, you, in effect, become a "faith parent" to your students, regardless of their age. Your students will ask you, as their teacher, "the meaning of the decrees and the statutes and the ordinances" of God. How do you feel about carrying on the task of your ancient forebears?

What do you think and feel about the command to teach for God?

Do you feel equipped and ready to explain the "meaning of the decrees"? How well acquainted are you with basic Christian beliefs? with the Bible?

What help do you need to feel well enough acquainted to do a good job as a teacher?

What helps are available from your church education leaders? (Workshops and training opportunities are typically offered in your district or conference, so be sure to ask your pastor to help you discover these options.)

Goals of Education

We already mentioned that one goal of religious instruction is to know God, and another is to teach the Law, that is, to help learners understand, know, and incorporate into their own religious identity the basic tenets of the faith. This is a fancy way of talking about faith formation.

A third goal of education is disciple making. Consider this instruction from Jesus to his own disciples and all disciples through the ages:

> All authority in heaven and on earth has been given to me. Go therefore and make disciples of all nations, baptizing them in the name of the Father and of the Son and of the Holy Spirit, and teaching them to obey everything that I have commanded you. (Matthew 28:18-20)

He further added the comforting reminder, "I am with you always, to the end of the age." Jesus does not ask his followers to do anything without providing them with help and assurance.

Disciple Making

The word *disciple* means learner. Jesus' disciples were his inner circle of learners, who taught and modeled the faith both with him and after him. When they moved into a more active role, they were referred to as apostles. *Apostle* means one who is sent. These first disciples helped gather other disciples, who taught and inspired other disciples, who invested themselves in forming other disciples, who through the generations later touched your life and made you a disciple. Now you have joined this generous line of learners in order to teach, lead, and nurture new disciples.

It is amazing and marvelous enough to imagine oneself in a two-thousand-year heritage in the history of Christianity, but it is even more amazing to realize that our ancestral line of faith goes back much, much further than even that. The urging in Deuteronomy 6 to teach one's children was put in written form in about the ninth century B.C., but it reflects a time four hundred years earlier. While no one can date when Moses received the Law from God, Moses is believed to have lived around 1250 B.C. God instructed the community to hand down the faith from their earliest days as a people—over thirty centuries ago!

Think about yourself as a disciple in a long line of

disciples—over three thousand years old! What feelings does this evoke for you?

Being a Disciple

Here you are, a teacher of Bible and faith, in a long line of others who have given of themselves to make disciples. What does that mean? First, look at the model of ministry of the first-century church. The earliest Christians following the Crucifixion and Resurrection

> devoted themselves to the apostles' teaching and fellowship, to the breaking of bread and the prayers. Awe came upon everyone, because many wonders and signs were being done by the apostles. (Acts 2:42-43)

As a result of this new, faithful way of living,

> the whole group of those who believed were of one heart and soul, and no one claimed private ownership of any possessions, but everything they owned was held in common. With great power the apostles gave their testimony to the resurrection of the Lord Jesus, and great grace

was upon them all. There was not a needy person among them, for as many as owned lands or houses sold them and brought the proceeds of what was sold. They laid it at the apostles' feet, and it was distributed to each as any had need. (Acts 4:32-35)

The teaching of the inner circle of Jesus' disciples, now apostles or leaders, inspired the converts to a new life that was shaped by
- teaching
- fellowship
- a common table and sharing of food
- corporate worship
- benevolent giving
- concern for the needy

Making Disciples

When we make disciples, we have a task greater than simply ensuring that our students know the Bible and what it means. The teaching task is a part of a wider, broader life that places each individual learner in a community that worships together, enjoys being together, extends itself on behalf of others, and seeks the welfare of the most marginalized and needy among them.

When either Jew or Gentile converted to Christianity, he or she had to learn not only the doctrines (core church teachings), but also the behaviors of this new community of faith. Many of them had to unlearn one way of life and learn a whole new way of life. As the early church forged new patterns of worship, of faith sharing, of relating to one another, they taught it all to newcomers.

The marks of this new life of discipleship were described and commented on often in the Bible, especially in the letters of Paul. Paul encouraged the congregation at Rome, for example, to

> let love be genuine; hate what is evil, hold fast to what is good; love one another with mutual affection; outdo one another in showing honor. Do not lag in zeal, be ardent in spirit, serve the Lord. Rejoice in hope, be patient in suffering, persevere in prayer. Contribute to the needs of the saints; extend hospitality to strangers.
> (Romans 12:9-13. See also verses 14-21 and Ephesians 4.)

For some people this orientation to life was quite foreign; they had to be taught by seasoned mentors.

Paul also observed that this community of faith is like a body with many members, each of whom has his or her own gifts, all to be used for building up the Kingdom (1 Corinthians 12:12-31; Ephesians 4:1-16). In accepting an invitation to education ministry, perhaps you are acknowledging or exploring your gift of teaching. It may be that someone else sees this spiritual gift in you and has named it for you.

As a teacher, you have the opportunity to observe, nurture, and name the spiritual gifts you see in others. As you do, you help others in the household of the saints identify their gifts and role in God's human family. The whole congregation, offering their gifts to God's purposes, works together in harmony to preserve the faith, grow the faith, and transmit the faith to future generations.

Think about the context from which you make disciples—the community of faith, the church. How does your church nurture, inspire, and challenge you to be a faithful disciple?

How do you see teaching and education in relation to worship, fellowship, giving, and service? (Remember the early church model in Acts 2 and 4.)

How does your participation in worship and fellowship opportunities help you grow as a Christian? as a teacher?

How does your contribution of gifts and personal service help you grow as a Christian? as a teacher?

Think about yourself when you were the age of your students (particularly if you teach children). How well did you understand various elements of worship, including what seem like the simple things, such as when to stand and when to sit, and what the special words and symbols mean?

In what ways might your teaching extend beyond what is in the printed lesson to help your students learn, at their own age level, what worship, fellowship, and service are all about?

Your Place in the Story

"If you can't preach like Peter, if you can't pray like Paul, just tell the love of Jesus, and say he died for all" (from the hymn "There Is a Balm in Gilead," African-American spiritual). You, like countless others through the centuries, have accepted the call to tell the story of Jesus. Remember, you are the latest participant in a history of over thirty centuries!

The story is rooted in the Bible and has numerous chapters. While we cannot tell the entire history of Christian education through the centuries in this booklet, we will mention a few highlights to help you see how your efforts contribute to the whole work.

Early Christian Primers: The Gospels

The Gospels are among the earliest documents for Christian education. Each of the Gospel writers had his own target audience and teaching agenda. The many long discourses and stories in Matthew serve a catechetical purpose; that is, they were a primer for new converts. Mark's tone is sometimes abrupt, typically concise, and usually urgent. In Mark's report, Jesus often acts "immediately." Luke shows a great concern by Jesus for the oppressed, the overlooked, and the outcast, and is often cited as the Gospel in which women play the most prominent role. One of John's emphases is on the signs or miracles, and he uses the most symbolism of the four Gospels.

As you teach from each of the Gospels, look for how the writer
- describes Jesus
- characterizes the disciples
- refers to other people
- uses stories
- uses symbolic language
- describes the relationship of Jesus with the Jewish authorities and non-Jews

How might these details help you explain the lesson better to your students?

Church Education

In the first several centuries of the Christian era, church leaders strongly emphasized catechism (core religious content). Converts were considered catechumens, learners who were to receive a particular religious instruction leading to baptism, inclusion at the sacrament of Holy Communion, and participation in the wider fellowship of the church. Prior to the serving of Holy Communion, these learners departed the worship service for private instruction in the beliefs and creeds. Instruction was oral and relied heavily on memorization. When the learners had mastered a certain core of beliefs, they were welcomed, typically on Easter, in the sacrament of baptism followed by Holy Communion.

Think about the purposes of the lessons you teach. (The purposes are often stated in the lesson, especially for children and youth.) How can you both teach the lesson material (content) and see the activity in the context of making disciples?

Teaching Through the Arts

For many centuries, most average citizens were illiterate. This was particularly true during the Middle Ages in Europe. As a consequence, passing on the faith relied greatly on artistic, rather than literary, means. This era brought the advent of the passion play; narrative decoration in church windows and architecture; and icons and symbols in altarware, clergy vestments (ministerial garb), and paraments (church furniture garb). Music and ritual were important educational tools as well, as both helped establish memorized patterns and beliefs.

You and your students have your own preferred learning and teaching styles, which are discussed and described in other volumes of this series. In looking at your lesson material, how much does it draw on music, drama, and the other arts? How can you use or add those creative methods to enhance your lessons?

Teaching the Bible

People in religious orders (monks and nuns) were more likely to be literate. Bibles were painstakingly copied by hand and elaborately decorated and illustrated. Eventually, Europe lifted itself to greater levels of education and literacy. The invention of the printing press, no doubt one of the most valuable contributions in the world's history, opened the way to widespread ownership and readership of the Bible.

How much of your lesson material prompts the direct use of the Bible?

Think about Scriptures you have learned and remember well. How have they helped you cope with various situations in your life? How can you help your students, at their age level, learn foundational Bible verses that carry them through the trials and joys of life?

The Protestant Reformation

The church has grown through the centuries but has experienced its own low spots, weaknesses, and lapses in following biblical teachings. Church leaders, such as John Calvin and Martin Luther in the sixteenth century and John Wesley in the eighteenth century, called for various reforms to bring the church more closely in alignment with the Gospel. In some instances these reformers and change agents rebelled against Roman Catholic belief and practice and encouraged greater reliance on reason, rather than emotion, in the practice of their faith. One consequence was a reduced emphasis on ritual and a greater emphasis on the Bible. Unfortunately, one thing sacrificed on the altar of reform was much of the artistry of the teaching and worship.

Look at your church sanctuary. Is the room plain, or does it use banners, altarware, or other visual means of conveying God's presence? Look at your classroom. Are there ways to enhance the space with art or other tangible items that will also help you teach your lessons? What might you add?

The Sunday School

Since the late 1700's the church and community have benefited from the creation of the Sunday school, led by Robert Raikes in Gloucester, England. Originally intended as a means to teach poor children to read and thus to learn their catechism (remember the early church catechumens?), the Sunday school movement eventually moved from secular instruction to only religious instruction. The church, however, has been heavily invested in both Christian and secular education for centuries. Many schools, colleges, and trade schools owe their beginnings and current support to church or synagogue. An important function of much mission work around the world involves teaching, whether the instruction is in the Bible, village management, farming, economic development, health care, or a wide variety of other subjects. From before God's call to Moses, God has urged the people of faith to learn about God and to carry on God's message and work throughout the world. And so we come to you.

Your Place

You have a place in this heritage; and in your own way, you make your mark on human history. Recent research on the sufficiency of curriculum resources suggests that the teacher is seven times more important to the success of a class than are the resources used in the class. Remember that there are several millennia's worth of ordinary people who precede you who took up the task of teaching with the gifts and tools they had at their command and did the best they could. Since the church continues, obviously they had significant success. You can, too. God desires to be known, and thus desires your success. Jesus instructed his disciples in the essential story, and the Holy Spirit strengthens us and reminds us of all Jesus taught. You don't have to regard yourself as Moses or Paul; you just have to be faithful and diligent. Even those heroes of the faith had to start at the beginning and learn at their own parents' and teachers' knees.

Going Further

In these brief pages it is possible to mention only a few of the people and events that have been instrumental in our Christian heritage. As you seek to learn more, one place to begin is your local congregation. If you ask questions and listen to the experiences of others, you will find a rich local heritage of stories of how people in your community have lived as God's people. As with the ancient Hebrews, these stories will tell of times when God's covenant was kept and times when it was broken. A few questions you may want to explore are

- How and why did my congregation start?
- What are the stories that are told when the congregation gathers?
- What symbols are present in my church? What do they represent?

- What events are held each year? How did they start? Why are they important to the congregation?
- How has the congregation been in mission and ministry in the past? How have these ministries changed over the years?
- How are the sacraments of baptism and Holy Communion celebrated in my congregation?
- Who are the saints, both alive and dead, who have helped to form the disciples in my congregation?

The resources in the following section will also provide additional information as you learn more about our Christian heritage and claim your place in the long line of disciples who continue to pass the faith to others.

Helpful Resources

Websites

General Board of Discipleship of The United Methodist Church (www.gbod.org). On this site you will find articles related to discipleship and teaching. Particular sites of interest are www.gbod.org/education and www.gbod.org/keepingintouch.

Discipleship Resources (www.discipleshipresources.org). In this online bookstore you can purchase additional copies of this booklet, other booklets in the series, and other books published by Discipleship Resources.

Christian History.Net (www.christianitytoday.com/history/). This website has a wide variety of articles related to Christian heritage.

Books

Church History in Plain Language, by Bruce L. Shelley (Word, 1996). An easy-to-read survey of Christian history.

The Meaning of Holy Communion in The United Methodist Church, by E. Byron Anderson (Discipleship Resources, 2000). An introduction to the United Methodist understanding of the sacrament of Holy Communion.

The New Oxford Annotated Bible, New Revised Standard Version, edited by Bruce M. Metzger and Roland E. Murphy (Oxford University Press, 1994). A study Bible that includes informational footnotes, cross-references, Bible maps, an abbreviated concordance, and other study helps.

The Spiritual Formation Bible, edited by Timothy Jones (Zondervan, 1999). Available in both the New Revised Standard Version and the New International Version. Includes devotional helps.

Ordering Information

Resources published by Discipleship Resources may be ordered online at www.discipleshipresources.org; by phone at 800-685-4370; by fax at 770-442-9742; or by mail from Discipleship Resources Distribution Center, P.O. Box 1616, Alpharetta, GA 30009-1616.